Fort Bragg &
Other Points South

OTHER BOOKS BY ROSEMARY DANIELL

Sleeping with Soldiers: In Search of the Macho Man
Fatal Flowers: On Sin, Sex and Suicide in the Deep South
A Sexual Tour of the Deep South (Poems)

Fort Bragg &

Other Points South

Poems by
ROSEMARY DANIELL

An Owl Book
Henry Holt and Company
New York

for Zane, the soldier who wore my perfume
with his camouflage fatigues while I was away

Copyright © 1968, 1969, 1977, 1979, 1982,
1983, 1985, 1986, 1987, 1988 by Rosemary Daniell
Published by Henry Holt and Company, Inc.,
115 West 18th Street, New York, New York 10011.
Published in Canada by Fitzhenry & Whiteside Limited,
195 Allstate Parkway, Markham, Ontario L3R 4T8.

Library of Congress Cataloging-in-Publication Data
Daniell, Rosemary.
Fort Bragg & other points South.
"An Owl book."
I. Title. II. Title: Fort Bragg and other points
South.
PS3554.A56F67   1988   811'.54   87-32095
ISBN 0-8050-0692-3 (pbk.)

First Edition

Designer: Lucy Albanese
Printed in the United States of America
10 9 8 7 6 5 4 3 2 1

*Grateful acknowledgment is made to the editors of the following publications in which these
poems first appeared:*

The American Voice, no. 5 (Winter 1986): "Fort Bragg"; *The American Voice,* no. 3
(Summer 1986): "Loss of the Soul & Other Sicknesses"; *Arrival* (Summer 1987):
"Craving Hollywood"; *The Chattahoochee Review,* vol. 5, no. 3 (Spring 1985): "A
Pile of Chopped Pine Logs"; *The Chattahoochee Review,* vol. 5, no. 4 (Summer
1985): "Sex in Savannah," "A Lisp for Myth Amerika"; *Contemporary Southern
Poetry, An Anthology,* edited by Guy Owen and Mary C. Williams (Louisiana State
University Press, 1979): "Of Jayne Mansfield, Flannery O'Connor, My Mother &
Me"; *The Great Speckled Bird,* vol. 2, no. 8 (1969): "Make Your Own Napalm,"
"The Distant War," and "A French Kiss for Inez Garcia"; *Negative Capability,* vol.
2, no. 4 (Fall 1982): "Sewing Lesson" (under the title "Sewing"); *Negative
Capability,* vol. 7, nos. 1 and 2 (1987): "Valentine's Day, 1982"; *Paintbrush,* vol. 10,
nos. 19 and 20 (Spring and Autumn 1983): "The Color of Halcyon Days,"
"Yellow Birds"; *Poem,* nos. 3-4 (November 1968): "The Wild Birds"; *Southern
Poetry Review,* vol. 16 (1977): "Of Jayne Mansfield, Flannery O'Connor, My
Mother & Me"; *Sweetwater Southern Poetry Series,* vol. 1 (1976): "The Wild Birds";
Woman Poet—The South, an anthology edited by Elaine Dallman, to be published
in 1988: "A French Kiss for Inez Garcia."

ISBN 0-8050-0692-3

Contents

Fort Bragg

The Color of Halcyon Days

• *This symbol is used to indicate a space between stanzas of a poem wherever such spaces are lost in pagination.*

Of Jayne Mansfield,
Flannery O'Connor,
My Mother & Me

CRAVING HOLLYWOOD

for Peyton, and my friends in The Program

1

Daddy
you were a slave to booze: no-good
& to the Southern doghouse born—
hiding behind your newspaper
the World War you couldn't get into—
on your miniature golf course
amid your Victory tomatoes—
driven by Jim Beam to get
out of the house   to the garage—
away from Mother   the tragic
queen   your wronged belle   me   the ice
princess   your little brown maid. . . .

For a long time   Daddy   we were
a threesome: you in your felt
fedora   Mother in high-heeled pumps
me   (not yet cuffed or collared)
in fur muff   patent Mary Janes—
tapping off to catch the newsreels
Dana Andrews   Claudette Colbert
The Purple Heart or *Since You Went
Away*   & Daddy   more & more
you did   squeezing yourself into
that bottle   glass all around   as
cut off as any ship   Daddy
I've got to hand it to you: you
left home without even traveling

3

2

now   forty years later   I crave
like Diane Keaton in *Annie Hall*
the shallows of L.A.   the sun
a warm Jacuzzi   but instead
my brain   like Woody's   plunges me
to murky pools   those waterworks
I feared at nine as   Daddy   you
swerved the Ford from curb to curb
as Mother screamed in the night   as
I clutched baby Anne   my talisman. . . .

& no safety   it seems   is enough
to allow me the shallows of
California   the sun   a warm
Jacuzzi: no matter how perfect
the set   how plastic the trees
how clear   blue-bottomed the pool

I can think only of drowning:
Daddy   wherever I go   you
float   tiny man in your   bottle:
always out of reach   yet casting
your shadow   marring everything.

SEWING LESSON

TUCKER, GEORGIA, CIRCA 1955

When I was fourteen   I made a sun dress
of pink waffle piqué.   The pattern was by
Vogue & complicated: scallops at the hem
scallops at the neck   scallops on the sleeves
scallops at the base   of the short pink jacket—
each round form traced   cut   sewn   reversed with
a special tool from Woolworth's: I made
it to perfection
                        wore it on my first
date with the boy   who became my first
husband   & when he whispered   "Are you
a Christian?"   I giggled   dreaming my neat
secret genitals.   & somehow the neatness
of my sewing   my virgin thighs sweetly
folded   had to do with pink piqué
inversions   with the rightness of all
perfect things
                        & that year & the next
sewing saved me: I made clothes
to wear on dates: a red corduroy
skirt & vest   a long-sleeved red plaid shirt
flaming   to match the pimples with which
I was beginning to break out   next
an Easter suit—navy & white checked
wool: wearing it downtown to the show
with the boy who became my second
husband   I noticed the pleats still held
the basting threads   my acne was raging
my grades at school falling   my parents
really into their fights.   As things

got worse   my sewing fell off: a gold wool
jersey blouse I had worked on for weeks had
an ugly buttonhole that couldn't be fixed
a gray wool jersey skirt had a raw
protruding seam   in the next dress I made
in home ec   I felt like a walrus beneath
the gathers & pleats
                        I now had a rule:
all clothes were to be thrown into the
corner of my room   the gray skirt worn only
on Mondays & Thursdays   the red corduroy on
Tuesdays & Fridays   the ugly blouse on
Wednesdays.   I scorched my cheerleading
sweater on the heat register   lost
a boyfriend when he found out I wore
falsies
        things were getting worse & worse:
Daddy was threatening me with knives   Mother
was sobbing & slobbering   the Baptist preacher
was complaining   the first boy & the second
were making me choose—
                      so forgetting how neat
my insides were   I married each of them
in succession   & didn't sew anything
       for fifteen years.

A LISP FOR MYTH AMERIKA

*for Ms. Vanessa Williams,
with tongue in cheek*

Lying in a bed in
the Days Inn outside
Fredericksburg   we
watch Bert Parks swish
out of twirling
lips   as down
the starry brights
prance the ten
chosen by personal
interview to find
out which is best
at giving head:
"I can!"   lisps
the miss from Texas
"the final syllables
of A-mer-I-Kan."
Last year's queen
her body a temple
for Christ   trips out
in whorehouse red:
"I believe every-
one in this great
country has a chance
if *he* wants it!"
The governor of New
Jersey rises   behind
him   the judges—
Lance Loud   Rock
Hudson.   Wearing
the same hairdo

I wore at nineteen
the girls grin through
Vaseline   especially
Miss Hawaii   forced
to wear a lei to
set off her difference.
Beside my Jewish
lover   who himself
prefers shiksas
I strain for a way
to drain your living
color   but Miss
Amerika   Myth
Amerika   in your
sarcophagus by
Magnavox   your gown
by Henry Ford
you stare at us
as though your teeth
might break   & it takes
a long time   God
a long time   for your
sad smile to fade. . . .

O corpse of my
little sister
how can you hope
to escape   through
the right shade of
lip gloss   the loss
of a single pound
what will happen
when you turn forty
what crawls between
your darling thighs?

A FRENCH KISS FOR INEZ GARCIA

for Joan Little, Yvonne Wanrow, * and my
seven-year-old niece, running from her
fifteen-year-old Bible-toting molester

Women are born through warm
water: my sister sucked
her thumb   loving the damp
my sobs soaked sheets   drove
husbands insane   & Inez   it's said
you have long wet beds: in-
stead of a Chicano   Miss
Alexander   (fluffy wigs
plum-smeared lids)   you're
Barbie turned Didee   poly-
vinyl with a leak.   Inez
when the prosecutor pressed
urine ran down your legs
spread over newsprint fed
by Randolph Hearst   to Repub-
lican judges   to crewcut
plainclothesmen   to all the male
shrinks who tell us   wetting
is anger repressed.   Yet

Inez   I flash the moments
in which your incontinence
ceased   when with a Burnt Pink
finger   you pulled the trigger
as   in a courtroom   you spewed
"Let the judge be raped—
see how *he* likes it!"   &
sister   merwoman   see you now
arms deep in prison tubs of

9

dishes or laundry   soaked for
the Patty Hearsts of this world
yet rising   rising from steam
in your state-issued dress—
& dream   trashed dolly   dark
Jeanne d'Arc   of how I might
rock you gently   undress &
redress you   of how we might
move together   you in
California   I in Georgia
all women   washed-out   third
world   poor white   to form
at last   a wall of tears
a tidal wave of rage.

*A Colville Indian woman from Spokane, Washington,
Wanrow was convicted by an all-white jury of second-degree
murder and first-degree assault for defending herself and her
son against a known child molester and rapist.

OF JAYNE MANSFIELD,
FLANNERY O'CONNOR,
MY MOTHER & ME

for Alice Walker, whose blackness
made the enemy visible

Myth of the Spanish moss:
within each hard tree   a bound
woman writhes: her hair   twists
of ash   claws   crawls the air. . . .
in Milledgeville   live oaks
blanch the Blood of the Lambs—
debs in white cotton panties
crimped matrons in slips of white
lace   all the permanent Daughters
of the Confederacy   caught
in their corsets of white
brocade.   Yes   this is an ash
blonde town   the white satin
undergarment of the Baptist
Belt   of swamps where white
crewcut sheriffs run down blacks
& women.   It's three A.M.

& I lie in the John Milledge
Motel   room 4D   where Jayne
Mansfield slept   a half-mile
down Highway 441
from the white town house where
Flannery stitched the white
home ec apron required for her
graduation from the same
school where my mother wore
white middy blouses   wrote on

white notebook paper   "I want
to marry a lawyer   live in
a house with white columns. . . ."

& trying not to hear   through
white walls   the sounds of white
male cursing   I think Jayne
her white satin hair spreading
her white plastic breasts rising
beneath this cover of white
chenille   the white white sperm
of half of Amerika   gliding
across her light pancaked cheeks—
& imagine Flannery   sweet
between her white girl's sheets
watching upon a white white
ceiling   blank white pages
the petits fours with white icing
of literary teas   & now flash
my mother   her Pond's palms
pressed against her magnolia
petal face   dreaming the blonde
man who would save her   the white
white roses   the white satin
wedding   the honeymoon trip.

Yet listening to the *mother
fuckers   sons of bitches*
the brute motel plans made by
white southern men   I wonder:
did Jayne see already   her
decapitation on a dark road
outside New Orleans   her head
that Clairol-pale egg   severed
as in life from her body?

Or did Flannery   Catholic &
weird   feel even then the wolf
disease   eating out her teen
age limbs: the falling hair
melting hipbones   the hospital
cuff   tightening   tightening?

& did my mother   even before
my Cherokee-tinged father—
the drinking & the gambling—
the bills & torn underwear—
sob into her dormitory
pillow   bubbling within her
belle's brainpan with the
lobotomies of marriage
the electrodes for shock   her
suicide at sixty?   Yes

did each of them: Jayne
her throat neatly stitched
Flannery   her face turned
moony by cortisone   my mother
whitened to wax by Revlon
her upper lip bleached blonde
wearing her best white gold
costume jewelry   yes   did
each of them know   lying
in this white satin–lined
sarcophagus for women   that
the first drop of blood ruins
the crotches of white cotton
panties   spots the slips of
white nylon lace   stains the backs
of white wedding dresses   yes
turns each of us scarlet women

deserving of mutilation
disease   damnation   that we
like the women in the trees
are embalmed   & recalling
my rage   washing between pale
blue lines   the blood-black scrawl
of my mother's girlish plans
I wonder what sleep awaits me—
freak of cunt & brain   in this
place   pure   white   chaste.

Sex in Savannah

SEX IN SAVANNAH

"In this room *fag hag* five
out of six people
have had Norman"
comments Howard
who was number two.

Looking carved by
Michelangelo
Norman chugalugs
Maddog 20-20
from the inside
vest pocket of
his three-piece mint
green suit as
Violet in violet
crepe   once a forty
ish man   sports
the tits of a seven
teen-year-old   chats
it up with Miss
Cherry Delight who
spreads sperm on
his cheeks each night
"for the complexion
my dear   & oh yes
I *al*ways use a sun
screen: PF 15."

In a soft lapel
jacket   as tender as

a rabbit's   Steven
bleeds Rive Gauche scent
ravishing red eye
shadow   bleats how
he lives in a pent
house in the Essex
two roommates   sex
indeterminate   that
now he is just
passing through on
his way to Acapulco. . . .

"He *ust* to live
in a dump on Haber
sham   would fuck
anything that moved!"
whispers Howard who
last read his poems
grinning through wounds
made by "some Marines
who drug me over
the Carolina line
scraped my body all
over with broken
Heinekens bottles. . . ."

now nudges Joey
who in braces &
Docksiders   fresh
from Daddy's money
the Hotel Chelsea
the School of Visual
Arts   giggles
·

and in a grace
to the only true
cunt in the place
Miss Cherry Delight
puts her hand
up my skirt
Steven tugs at
my fuck-me pumps
pumps the zipper
to Norman's fly
while Joey   on
the floor   kisses
Violet open-mouthed

"Joey   you've got
stretchmarks on your back"
Norman protests—
pulls me from this
nest of pink worms
squirming on the fake
Oriental   & like

Mercury   we slip
to Dr. Feelgood's
where pierced by sexual
strobe lights   narcissistic
neon   we sniff a jump
start for the heart
a hedonist's digitalis—
now move through dry ice
fogs   gayly push back
the night   our deaths

ILLEGAL ENTRY

for yet another John

Two A.M.   I open my eyes
a black panther   fangs bared   rises
an inch from my lashes: when we
plunged onto this bed   I didn't see
your tattoo   thick with black ink
flick of red tongue   eyes of gold
instead   I had been searching
your cool blue ones   listening
between kisses   thrusts   licks
to the stories of your crimes—
breaking & entering   aggravated
assault   then   a heroin addict
now   here in Savannah   the Army
Dr. Feelgood's where we danced   where
I caressed your neck ("my most
erotic spot")   let you feel
me up each time we twirled close
where you murmured   "If I
had a room   I'd take you there."
Instead—I took you to mine
a skinny blond boy in jeans   &
now you tell me of your marriage
to Audrey   the fights   the two
year-old   of sweltering in
your job as a welder   next
of your sexual fantasies
the real orgies you've been to—

all this with your body within
mine   breaking & entering

again & again: you want
to tie me up next time
you say   & if I'm afraid
you'll let me go first.   It's easy
to tell you my own flash of
lying on the table for the
Eucharist   fucked from a distance
by a priest with a candle
tied to a long stick   or the more
mundane one   two men at once.

How 'bout *more* than two   you ask
my Army buddies?   a gang bang?
I should be freaked out at that
& all the rest you've said
not to speak of the switchblade
open at the head of the bed—
so why do I feel instead
as peaceful as a baby
afloat in her mother's arms
that this lovelessness is what
freedom is   that having you
this way   ghetto boy   is
the danger that will save me?

CRUISING IN SAVANNAH &
OTHER POINTS SOUTH

1

The sensualist's hell:
every Tuesday night
at exactly 11:08
you will pick up a new trick.

Every Tuesday night
for the next ten years
pick up a stranger
move back one space:

2

I stand at the bar
my silk shirt unbuttoned
the space between my breasts
smeared with Tatiana

you have on a plush
shirt I want to touch
jeans signed by Sasson—

insta-sex credo:
if you're wearing these
clothes   you're probably
not a murderer

my glossy lips part   curve
toward the dark curls
that bubble at your throat

or is it dried blood
flaking in coils?

toward you   the stranger who
holds my light   who
cups my hand in yours

knowing that in an hour
the gold chain at your neck
will drag across my lips—

"sport-fucking"   it's called—
like skydiving or hang
gliding   a high-risk sport
a way of sliding past

a sickening sweet   like
trudging through fields of
chocolate-covered cherries

a way of finding out
that sex is slippery
& cannot penetrate

that sex is speechless
despite its given names

that not having sex   is
like talking with   one's
mouth taped   Oh!

it's the happy hour!
bar scotch   two-for-one:
for what we do   booze   coke
vitamin Q are the drugs

prescribed   fogs to erase
the stigmata of our order—

to numb just enough to let us
say it with flesh   it says
more than roses   better than
milk toast in bed   or some
thing from the oven   more
soothing than Vicks VapoRub—
steak to an endless bruise:

your ex took your kids
to California   & you're
so lonely   you had a girl
but she's dying of cancer—
nine months ago   I had
someone I could have loved
carved from my womb like
the core from an apple:

now we share communion
sip funereal spirits   &
I'm so happy I could die
flashes across the bill-
bored of my mind: *monogamy?*
or was it *monotony* you said?
and *tied down:*   were you asking
whether I liked it?   Or saying
you don't want to be?

though being forced to all
fours   ridden like a horse
bridled and whipped   would

barely be discipline enough
for the liberties we take

Yet sex   like pain   staves
off death: a vital sign
and sailors ashore for only
one night   we exchange thrusts
just as soon we will
in bed   where eating each
other out like sharks or mad
thrushes   (moles burrowing into
each other   archaeologists
on futile digs?)   your dumb
flesh will become poultice
to my raw darkness   and
tomorrow   we'll wake
exhilarated by the digging
yet knowing little more
than I did in the dream
of coming   than I do now
as I watch your lips part
to sip Chivas and water

yes   in this moment
before we even touch

yet knowing only that your
secret can never be known—
even if we live together
for twenty years   even if I
hold your hand after operations
even if I am with you
at the moment of your death.

GRIEF FOR THE DRUNKEN GOOD TIMES

for my friend John Paul

Remember that time
I called my ex from the bar
& fell down on the cobblestones

& later   near dawn
met a shoe salesman from Charleston
slept with him in my room   while
you   his straight pal   lay fully clothed
atop the covers on Miss Jane's bed?

& how   the next day
we laughed through hangovers at
the way   afloat on white chenille
he kept shiny black oxfords on
tall sentinels against your mouth?

& the time when   stoned on kamikazes
I necked in front of the crowd
with an eighteen-year-old   danced
on the stage with a drag queen—
holding up my dress mons-level
pirouetted without my panties on?

& do you recall
the night when the waitress wouldn't
bring our check   & we left anyway
& I wet my pants on River Street
then we all went to Dr. Feelgood's
where my male lover danced with my
female lover   Miss Jane   & she got
mad   burst the tires on my Fiat
left angry for the movie set?

.

& how   before long
in a house full of orchids
the scent of sinsemilla
with a cake with cabbage roses
she became your bride   & we
all jumped into a pool   with or
without wedding clothes on   & you
your pregnant wife   & I made love
in a bright white room . . . ?

Oh   I know they say that people
who drink are miserable.   But
I don't remember it that way:
we were more like lovely fish—
silver-finned, in our element. . . .

But all that—all that was before
the baby son you never saw
again   the man who retaught me
pain   before the booze dug fingers
deep inside our brains   clawing out
chunks   getting to the quick   before
sex turned to rage   good times to grief. . . .

& now   as chaste
as a Jane Austen heroine
I read novels   drink tea in bed
& at times   from my window   watch
you walk home from the grocery
an aging man with your one bag—
& wonder if you feel as I do:

oh God   I pray never to be
that way again.   Oh God   I want
                              those old days back!

FUNERAL FLOWERS

APRIL 1976

for W.S.

1

*In Jackson Square   snake flowers
quiver: purple petals flicker—
priapism of the tongue   yes*

*I've got a lover in New
Orleans: when he looks down
on me   he always trembles.*

2

Mardi Gras: the stranger bares
a breast tattoo radiant—
a tit pierced by gold—
O God of the cobalt
eye   how did this come
to be: that one would
sit   allow the needle
passed through a nipple
next   the ring of metal—
the brute jewel by which
she is forced to her knees. . . .

3

You shed a shirt thick
with scarlet flowers   love
I stitch your chest   a
thousand scarlet flicks—

it's been six months   &
in the Heart of Columbus
on the Alabama line
we dissolve the time
between in plastic cups
of booze   & because of
the moon   my rhythms
move through pools of blood—
God   it's as though
my heart or yours had
burst upon the sheets:

the hotel linens wave—
fields of sudden poppies
& the next day   leaving
stains everywhere   I feel
beneath my satin blouse
beneath my Revlon mouth
the wound in my chest where
your heart lay.   Love
a displaced nipple   a needle
through a tit might sting
less than this.   & as
the miles pull like catgut
tow your plane toward New
Orleans   I dream I had cut
the thin red cloth to heart
shapes: sewn one over your heart
one over mine: bandages
to staunch   the absence of
your wrists: reminders of how
we are stitched to one
another   in embroidery of
blood   in blossoms of flesh.

4

Scarlet tulips: blood cups
pink azalea: tissue bared—

the world is a hospital room
full of flowers. We are the
bleeding: our wounds stand open.

5

Stems protrude my breastbone
red dirt rakes my blood
forsythia   forsythia   spring
in middle Georgia   & the boy
in the back row is sixteen
you are twenty-four   I am
thirty-eight   through the window
yellow screams   I look into
the faces of children at their desks—
think of you at yours in New
Orleans   over a staticky
radio   directing ships down
the Mississippi   a hippie's
job   love   if I could   I would
fall to the floor with this child
your likeness   enter into God
& madness   instead   I stand
reading poems   in a classroom
in Macon   while yellow forsythia
moan in rhythm   to what has
happened   is not happening

6

Macon: the Davis Brothers
Motel: you shove up my blue

crepe dress   me down to orange
acrylic   it's been six weeks—
your hair is longer now
curls over your neck.   In
the Waffle House on Georgia
475   you bend
over coffee: I flash you
genuflecting in Saint Louis
Cathedral   sipping communion
between the priest's legs—
"an effeminate heterosexual"
your gay friends call you—
the only man I've known who
dreams of angels   last night
I loved most the curve of your
spine that can belong only
to a man not yet thirty—
how is it that you with your
worries about your eternal
soul   your nipples like pink crepe
myrtle buds   can nail me
through mine   abscess after abscess?

7

Atlanta: you thrust the pint
into the pocket of your old
tweed jacket   your copy of
Saint Teresa into my hand—
pick up your bag   walk toward
Greyhound.   Yesterday   in
the Georgian Terrace   Church
full of pimps   whores   us
you became my priest   last week
in Savannah   in the John
Wesley Hotel   you cried
in the shower as I talked

31

on the phone   yet back in
our room   jerked me to my
knees by the ring through my
tit: Jesus   when we began
I was afraid of hurting *you*. . . .

8

The night we met   you wore
a black leather jacket   tiger
painted on the back   & later
in the Quarter   thinking we'd
never meet again   got drunk
robbed at knifepoint   the dynamite
jacket taken: "laid out just
this way"   you tell me as we
step over a wino: blood smears
the bar steps   the geeks were here
last night   bringing their cock
fights   we've been drinking
fifty-cent martinis   the noon
light scratches   I'm going
back   we both know it.   "Even
here"   you whisper   "romantic
love is carrion. . . ."   today
as that first day   New Orleans
is a tissue   suppurating
flowers   yet that was flesh
enflamed   this is flesh erupting:
azalea   enraged labia—
dogwood   stiff with blood
tips: everywhere   every-
where   blossoms thick as pus

9

July: the dead queen of the
Gulf: "like walking through hot
water   a funeral parlor"
you write me in New York—
outside the Chelsea   the stink
of garbage rises   in August
you warn   "while you're up there
getting famous   I'm fucking
my way up the entire West
Coast   we could have lived
together   but this is what
you wanted   isn't it?"
isn't it?   the husband who
told me to *stop* or "you'll lose
both of us"   smokes across
the room: when did the curls
of his chest   the curves of
your wrists   become the twin nails
hanging me my mine   O Christ
with his whip   Mary with her
curled lip   when did what was
pleasure start to turn to pain?

10

The day after Mardi Gras
one year ago   the priest
pressed the ashes deep into
our foreheads   today I walk
beneath *Jeanne d'Arc*   who   slick
blue   manless   withheld
even her menstrual blood—
yet mine weeps: in the bar

at the Fairmont   your hair
curls above your collar   you're
more handsome than I recall
an assistant professor now
have one girl   you tell me
a student of seventeen   her
whole skin surface perfect—
another who reads Proust
behind a sailor's bar   who
on the nights she will come
to you   leaves on your doorstep
a labia-pink seashell. . . .
you hold my hand in yours
murmuring something about
"coming to Atlanta sometime.". . .

11

in the limousine   forsythia
whiz by screaming   I gave
you up   my husband left
anyway   within the breast
you pierced   something grabs—
in the airport   on the plane
I vomit the taste of ashes
of rotting flower flesh

12

yellow violets: lymph clotted
scarlet tulips: blood stained
pink azaleas: tissue scarred
the world is a funeral room
full of flowers   we are the
dead   our wounds are sealed.

& JUST A LITTLE FURTHER
SOUTH

of Charleston   of Savannah
Of Islamorada Key   of
New Orleans   of Corpus
Christi   of the Baja

is Mexico & Guatemala
& Belize & Costa Rica—

all those places we go
to let the IQ sink to 60
the brain to the genitals

to sit & sip a rum soda
listen to a jukebox play
"Moon over Carolina"—

all the places we go
at the end of our tether:

this is the Park Hotel
these   the girls of San José
& south of here is Colombia
Peru   Chile   Argentina

though Incan   not as pretty
the girls there are cheaper
to show their price in Norte
Americano dollars   they
hold up hand calculators—

•

yes   it rains & rains here
& everything is rotting
yet the further south we go
the further south we yearn
to be   deeper in these tropics
this abandon   *abandon*   *abandon*
that we   *the adrift*   *call heaven.*

The Camoufleur

THE CAMOUFLEUR

Your brute blue eyes
stare down into mine
loosening my loins
despite the child
you've embedded there—

a soldier   "a trained
killer"   yet between
my legs turns wet
the flesh forgetting
that within three days
what it now cradles
will be scraped   shredded
whatever "dilatation
& curettage" does. . . .

> *he is the blond father of the dark baby*
> *thin   strong   tenacious   kicking her belly*
> *from within   but he   the killer   is stronger*
> *with his fist   his sex   his smile   he pummels her*

now to cheer me   you sit
on my side of the bed
tell a joke about
a dismembered frog—
all night   I dream
the wounded amphibian

& in the waiting room
for surgery   you laugh
about the gyn who held

at your ex-wife's vulva
a cigarette dripping ash. . . .

afterward   from my
bed table   the cool pink
flowers in green glass
call out to me of pity:
I want my dead mother!

but what I have is
the soldier   the comforts
of hard sex: you sit
beside me in rough
khakis   the gold
of your beard glistens
like metal   or chains
clanking   your biceps
beneath coarse cloth turn
turn my belly liquid. . . .

> *his hand at my throat   the other in my hair*
> *he twists   yanks   pounds   pounds my skull against*
> *now throws   throws me hard   my spine cracks. . . .*

& once more   I
draw you to me—
the camoufleur who
conceals within
the folds of my
peignoir   the strength
of the wrists   the
steel of the thighs
with which I will
clamp you   locking
your cock into place

driving the sperm
inward   forcing you
to my dirty work—

the bruises on my
breasts radiate
mauve   rose   yellow
the marks of a foreign
power   & I watch
as between my legs
you change   harden
becoming my own
SS man   the macho
fiend who   possessed
of my devils   takes
on my rage as I swoon
pure   victim again. . . .

> the beating has the same rhythm as the dance
> as sex   the taste in my mouth as delicious—
> "a sick ticket"   what I wanted all those nights?

TURISTA

SAN MIGUEL DE ALLENDE, 1984

In this place   women carry flowers—
hyacinths   gladiolas   bougainvillea.
Smiling   always smiling   the men   full-lipped
sensuous   comb their hair to liquid
dance from the hip   while Maria & Juan
emote   drunken children   & above our heads
gasoline-filled balloons burst into flames:

this is the Festival of Marionettes
& the masks the revelers wear   fanged beasts
or devils   are less real than the finned fish
the muscular snakes that swim through   wrap
my brain   & the blood that flows the face
of Christ after Christ is less red than what
poured from my split forehead   your knuckles
as they splintered mirrors that night. . . .

As a child   I feared the crocodile   his
needled grin   but here   the skull's gaze
the lizard's face scare me less than yours does

Norte Americano   football player
soldier   & these demons are less menacing
than those that contort your blond brow   swing
in space like thick serpents   writhe from your brain
into mine   yes   I   the *mala mujer*
who carries   like a fetus   your guilt
am less afraid of the stranger who kicks
another to death at my feet at three A.M.

outside the Labyrinth than I am of you
the gringo I love   the gringo I fled: here

my dreams are matched in blood & flowers
the main causes of death are turista
& homicide   yet *I am safe   am saved.*

LOSS OF THE SOUL
& OTHER SICKNESSES

1

In Savannah   I lie
writhing   fever 102°
& next to the sweating
glass   the melting aspirin
the Indian woman whose
gaze I snapped in a town
in south Mexico stares
from the top of the stack.

Perdono Señora Perdono!
I cried as she leaped from
the parade of demons   rushed
from the side of the youth
dressed in fur & wolf fangs
the man with the dead squirrels
roped to his waist   to grab
at my Polaroid   to sob from
beneath a mask of gnarled wood
what I had stolen from her—
her life   even her soul.

Her eyes through the knotholes
were as tear-filled as mine
became   each of us at that
moment   longing to turn back
time.   But tonight   I wonder:

is it she whose white-hot
finger traces each small
bone of my spine   who turns

up the flame beneath my brainpan
who sticks these pins of fire
through belly   breasts   thighs?

2

Or did she see beyond my
silk blouse   Revlonned grin
my Gold Card membership in
the "You Can Do Anything" club
to my betrayal   like hers
by the Christ of the bright
blue robes   the spirit vacuumed
from my body at puberty—
then the husbands shed like
skins   the grown son given
up on   the boy-child sent
to suction   the men fucked yet
not loved: a garment stitched
to flesh   trailing behind
me   as stained as the rags of
the faithful   walking the cobble
stones on bloodied knees?

3

Yes   did she forgive me—
lucky Norte Americano
Our Lady of Instant Credit
Mistress of Metamorphosis—
& even if she did
can we women from twin worlds
each fathered by a cruel God
witness to daughters sacrificed
mothers to men & grief
ever forgive ourselves?

45

THE SINS OF THE MOTHERS

for Elsa

1

Until Papa told you better   you
paraded uniformed in the squares
of Trieste   screaming for Mussolini

with the others.   But you were only nine
then   & Papa   so erect & handsome
disappeared one day to die a death
of which you heard only cruel versions—

& you saw your once-elegant mama
sell her furs   even fish   for the sake
of bread   your pretty sister sew all night
in bad light for potatoes   & you too
were shot at by the Germans   riding
the railroads   took codes to the partisans.

Then the liberation: & you   dark-eyed
beauty   modeled gowns for a designer
uncle   became the roller-skating champion

of Italy!   Only to be betrayed again
this time by Amerika   a GI as
blond   as blue-eyed as Papa had been:
sailing away on a crest of promises
he left you   a good girl   big with child—
a thousand Jews a day lay dying
but for this worse shame   your uncle came
to beat you up   & for the sake of your name
that baby   you shaped yourself: to another
soldier   plains family   mother-in-law

of the midwestern U.S.   "Lucky"
you murmured   tamping down your years
to a lifetime of dinners at six
PX's   patios   & bridge games—
playing good wife to a good man
good daughter to father & priest

later to be blamed by the very son
for whom this mutilation had taken place
the man who lived only because of your
grievous offense: being a teenage
girl   meeting a cute guy   giving in . . .

2

you tell me as we sit at this kitchen
table   sip communion wine   & Elsa
I agree: we couldn't be more different—
you with your duty to the Catholic
the good   me with my vows to art & self

yet I too am given to firewalking
know how to keep my errors smoldering
red coals stoked to sizzle out any ease
"& you've never forgiven yourself"
you say now as I burst into tears
tell you of an abortion at a time when
I had a living to make   another child—

& earlier   fleeing a Bible Belt
battlefield as crazed as the Church
as Fascism   (parents fighting to the death)
didn't I mold *my* life to one man
at sixteen   for the sake of the son
I bore   marry another at twenty?
Didn't I plan *my* chores a week ahead

go to the Garden Club   wear little
hats?   & at thirty   as your son lived out
a corn-fed puberty   didn't I drive
each Saturday to the state hospital
send mine abroad to save him from drug
dealers   "Your fault"   agreed the therapist-
confessor when I too wanted to wear
a red leather miniskirt   dance in
the jelly lights with the others   & later
after I had lost two husbands to love
of that son   (thrown plates against the wall
so one daughter could go to college
screamed for the other's right to New York
& mistakes)   I *would* do those things. . . .

3

Yet Elsa   our bonds cut further   deeper
to when you & I first knew we were
eaten out at the core   the rotten cause
of everything: each worse   despite
a world in man-made flames   than any SS
officer or bomber of Hiroshima—

but sister . daughter   isn't what
we grieve   not our slight sins   but what was
early carved away   within sleep as deep as
lobotomy   in surgery as certain as
a castrato's: that devil   that wild child
that free girl inside ourselves?   Isn't
the penance we make not for our faults
but to our severed twin   teratoma
of clit & brain   the part of us that
still screams *out*?   Elsa   isn't what we share
not our shame   but the guilt of the victim
the survivor   our own overwhelming rage?

48

VALENTINE'S DAY, 1982

1

Red tulips
two thick lips   in a pot:
no more blood—

but bruises on my arm
needle tracks on my daughter's—

no outlet   no getting out:
just two thick lips
juicy in a pot

a red room   a pink one
screaming   *"blood   blood"*
a dream of tiny hands
reaching up   imploring

the petals become packets
plasma kept at ready
membranes to dam our horror:

last night   I heard eyes
popped out by a screwdriver
on *Donahue*   a mother
tells of her child who at two
tried to pierce her own
with scissors   who at ten
clawed & clawed them.   &

who would not crave dope
or blindness   when a massacre

or birth   a torn wrist or
perineum   look much the same

when outside our bodies
await the rusted blades
the thick two-lips of a rapist
red-brown as a menstrual stain?

2

None of this is true.   Or
at least   only half-true:
yes   the tulips are there
in a clear green vase
on the table   the news
as usual   is tragic
my arm *is* blue   bruised
the needle tracks do exist
a fetus has been killed

& in grief for that child
& for other things
my lover & I fought

& for her deeper loss
my daughter did shoot up

3

but what else is true
is: *joy*.   My lover
at table   his body as
juicy   as succulent
as the tulip stalks—

•

my daughter in a red robe
fresh blood coursing between
her thighs   spreads homemade
bread with strawberries   red
red jam—the coffee steams
toward the curved pink ceiling
Darlene   the pink-gray cat
purrs atop the creamy
afghan   its cerise roses—

4

& the truth   the truth about life is:
short of death   (& even then?)
the worst imaginable can happen
hematoma can swell every landscape

& still   the colors burst forth
a tamponade of the heart   as sunsets
did to captives at Auschwitz   & like
some twist of a sweet Möbius strip
things change & change & change:

one night   on a barstool
at Fort Bragg   my lover will
turn from whiskey & rage—
leaving the dream of drugs
for paint   my daughter will
cook for a huge family
I will fly to Costa Rica
with a Hermès   my lover
will die in a Nicaraguan
jungle   his naked belly
now breathing in & out
across the table will tear

through me from a litter
on the pages of *Time*
someone will send a gift
of tulips: pale pink   sky
centered   small yellow fists
screaming   "I am! I am!"
& on a bus in L.A.
a man in cutoff black
leather   flesh pierced by
metal & chains   will shyly
ask for the sports section
of *USA Today*   &
I will think how we are
connected one to another

5

how now the three of us sit
drinking coffee   looking
into the beauty that rises
from bulbs submerged yearlong
in a dark   hard   bloodless ground
the joy that leaps up & up
like light from a clerestory
designed by a god or a maniac
the red red   blood-red   & juicy
tulips   the passion I will dream
of for the rest of my life.

Fort Bragg

FORT BRAGG

for Zane, & the soldiers of the peacetime Army

They have come here   the beautiful
blue-eyed boys   the silken caramel or
chocolatey ones   voluntary
admissions off the streets of The Bronx
the dirt roads of Kansas   to be kept
in safe houses   like prisons or treatment
centers   in the beds with the hospital
corners   in the mess with three squares a day
in the bars with the go-go dancers who
nightly rotate to country   hard rock
disco   to the barracks where each evening
the Vietnamese from the Pizza Palace
sings out   "sub   soda   pizza   egg woll
fwied wice   postdated check-k-k . . ."   to be held
in the PX   the spouse center   the museum
with its life-size photos of our boys posting
the Stars & Stripes in Grenada   in the local
picture show where *Rambo II* plays on
all four screens   yes   "three hots & a cot"
you can't beat it: this is a homey affair
the dream of children brought up on Sly Stallone
Chuck Norris   & all those late-night movies
those dashing mercenaries   outlaws   &
heroes   John Wayne & John Wayne & John Wayne
the high of being a yank & all that. . . .

& oh!   the romance of the military!
twelve-mile road marches   heavy packs on backs
jumping from planes at a thousand feet
slack-rapelling from helicopters
sleeping on the hot sands of the Saudi

55

in the steaming jungles of Panama
yes   the glory of living among men
as cruel   as hard   as you aspire
to be   snapping to   saying *yes* sir!
dismantling   reassembling   pulling
the pin on   shooting off the heavy stuff
hacking through brush with a real bayonet
learning to forget that if this tank ignites
you   too   go up in flames   a sizzled thing. . . .

& yet   what an orgasm!   winning the way
you did on the football field   the way
you didn't with the girls back then   almost
all murder is committed by males under
thirty-five   it's said   & at times   the chants
of the kill   (those vows to ship you home to Mom
in a Glad bag!)   churning the froth of your rage
two or more of you stomp a queer to death
in Georgia   throw a girl off a bridge
in Monterey   yes   the handsome young men
& some sinewy old ones are held here
thinking they are learning to kill when
really   they are learning to die: of booze
or dope   of bullets or the electric chair

& now you whom I love are volunteered
here   thrall to the cult of war games   wired
into the male machine   you who were once
a breast-fed baby   your tiny fingers
clutching   unclutching a tit   who   a skinny
kid   was sure your ears were too big   who
freckled   sky-eyed   looked up at the clouds
girls' dresses   who cried when your daddy drowned
the puppies   yet still   you sat on his lap
loving the smell of his Luckies   the only
dad you had   & besides   when you went

to ride   he knew all the truckstops: you
who were this way until you were caught up
in the barroom   on the football field   until
you learned to break your own nose & others'—
you   now turned this hard stringy creature
this man with but one mission   "to protect you"

you say   & yes   don't we all want that—
me at my desk in Savannah   my daughter
in her lab in Denver   my sister at
Jazzercise in Atlanta   my niece in her
Laura Ashleys   her Calvin Kleins   the all-
female audience in town for *Donahue*
a little damage at Bloomingdale's   yes
the housewives watching their soaps   the gals
having pedicures at Narcissistic Nails—

"I wish there was a brothel for *us*"
a woman once said   forgetting the two
sexiest places in the world   high schools
& Army posts   those reservations packed
with the men who would have been truck drivers
oil riggers   carpet layers   the men we turn
ourselves on with   the ones who may stare
or even whistle   who say "ma'am" & have
instant hard-ons.   Yet except on the pages
of *Playgirl*   the stage with the "Peter Adonis
Show"   we won't look back at you   instead
are trained to cut you away in favor
of doctors   lawyers   stockbrokers: men
who are paunchy yet "interesting." . . .

& no   we don't want you to be our sons
we want you kept   exercised   well fed
in the compound   your brute strength put to this use
a ready sacrifice: during W.W. II

a German boy was shot so that an Italian
woman I know could live   & in the U.S.
at Neiman-Marcus   over bridge tables
consoled by the very priests who said *nothing*
of the death camps   she has lived as easily
with that as we who appease testy husbands
for charge accounts   & if soon   one or more
of you lie   guts spilled in a ditch in Honduras
we won't even know it   & what if we did?

At best   you will become a war hero
someone will make a movie about your kind
& dreaming   not our doughy spouses   but
Richard Gere   Mel Gibson   between our thighs
we will rush to watch you   for this is the real
triage: the ready spilling of the blood
of those who mean little to us   (farm boys
at Gallipoli   bank clerks at Verdun
auto workers in Vietnam)   a separation
that takes place long before any front is reached—
a meltdown in which all the ancient   endless
& hidden injuries of class coalesce

& darling   as surely as you   some starless
night   might cut away from your parachute
I will cut you away from me. Yet love
can't I   a toughened journalist   you
with your allegiance pledged   instead fall
together through that black hole into
a bright white-clouded place without guns
compounds   or dreams of glory   where you
again become the sky-eyed boy with big
ears   puppy   I   the little girl who
thinking him handsome   guilelessly loves
the little boy from across the tracks?

MAKE YOUR OWN NAPALM

      Rip free
the plastic that binds   the tops of
beer cans.   over a pan of water   with
tongs or pliers   hold it at arm's length.
light a match to the edge of the stuff:
hear it begin to screech   watch it melt
& drip   see it fall in blobs   like
fat   or flesh from muscle.   Observe
how the flame holds on like the teeth
of a dog gone rabid: a fire that makes
fritters of matter   that boils even the
fragments in water.   Yes   go now: make
your own napalm   & each night before
you sleep   dream how that flame
crawls   your skin   or your baby's

THE DISTANT WAR

OUTSIDE ATLANTA, 1967

At the kitchen sink
you cut through
a bunch of lettuce.
Your hand pushing leaves
you dream the brush of jungle:
greener   rough & stinging:
through the plumpness of your thigh
a sear runs like shrapnel

& you recall   how
at noon   women at the luncheon
ate Baked Alaska:
jeweled fingers moved spoons
toward mouths that
between bits of dripping sugar
dropped words like:
"War should be declared."

& a woman in a flowered hat
as wide as she
had a balloon from her mouth
that said
"Those men are not our kind . . .
we must protect our own ways. . . ."

like luncheons   like Baked Alaskas
like spoons & jeweled fingers.
Yet to you   in your kitchen
expansions of spices

rise to contain a sting:
loosed in the cut on your thumb
does the vinegar for salad burn
more than the metal that pours
through a boy's thigh through way of yours:
a burning he can't tear out of his skin
a burning you soon cannot tear out of yours

as you place the salad inside the bowl
as over coffee   you sit & read:
you   the well-read housewife reads:
on arts   *The Village Voice* states:
    Marc Morrell makes forms out of flags
    Marc Morrell stuffs the flag and chokes it with a rope
    Marc Morrell is charged   the gallery owner is charged
    perjury on those dead pieces of cloth
cotton is the dead flower of the cotton plant
the flag was made from cotton
killed   colored   dyed

ripped from their bolls
like leaves of lettuce
are ripped from their core

like boys are ripped from their lives.

& preparing the flesh
of a lamb for broiling
you watch interviews
on television: homefront opinions:
in a party hat of tinfoil
a patron of the local VFW states
"The killing of women and children is just a natural part of it"
  •

of war
our natural occupation
of war
our mass death wish
of war
thousands upon thousands of homosexual grapplings

Yet this moment   on your kitchen stool
sits your neighbor's son   not yet twenty
come to say good-bye   he tells you
he is not afraid   only of not being brave if captured
"My friend, you would not tell with such high zest
To children ardent for some desperate glory,
The old lie: *Dulce et decorum est*
Pro patria mori."

But your neighbor's son
hasn't read Wilfred Owen
& if he did   wouldn't believe it—
he only sits & talks
of guns   of mud   of the girls of Saigon

& you   listening
hear only his scream   noting
the hairs on his arm are as light as your baby's
the muscles lumps of semiprecious substance
to be kept from jungle sun and melting.
To be kept from hot places like wars.

The Color
of Halcyon Days

A PILE OF CHOPPED PINE LOGS

for James Dickey, long ago

1

On a Sunday in fall
in the gold backyard
you stare into a pile
of chopped pine logs—

and for some reason
recall one red leaf
the color of blood
on a sea of mud
near the edge of a foxhole:

the unbelievable shrapnel
of loneliness
was more real
than metal toward your chest.

And now   gazing into the logs
chopped and stacked for winter fires
you think how each is centered
by a core like yours: each
bound in rings as hard as wood
only to be released to the power of ash.

2

And Monday morning
you rise at five

glance at the shape
of your sleeping wife—
see a new hair of gray
a fresh line engraved:

strange   unnoticed
on a woman whose arm
has crossed your chest all night
as though bridging some gulf—

and you recall
how   the night before
the dishes done
the kitchen yellow
you laughed together
at a funny saying
of the baby's: for hours
you dreamed you knew her.

3

But today is the day for a business trip—
you must rush to a jet that will rise
forty thousand feet   when endless space
and depth will become your metaphor:
you   hurled through your time on earth
surrounded by strangers   and helpless.

And later   you will rise on an elevator
with twenty others: twenty floors
you will go together: bodies touching
yet packed in cases of pure   unending
separation   each watching only
for the electronic light of a number.

4

At the kitchen table
you now begin
the morning news—
what rushes in
                    between
            the paper and your eyes?

Another's pain   another's death
is only a photograph: flat   unreal
a symbol on cheap newsprint.

5

And while the coffee perks
you walk as drawn to the room
of your son   who twists in dreams
that you can never dream   or know:

his body breathes a life only his—
already   thrusting toward a future
when you are gone: the creation
of an unconsciousness
far beyond yours alone.

6

You recall how   at his birth
you held her hand   helpless:
though you had given seed and gene
knowing you could never share
her red dream of pain   the dark
corridor of birth   the journey
of a child who traveled slowly
and alone:

                    as she left you
for a sleep
deep in Demerol
you left   relieved

to pass a nearby room
to hear a doctor tell a woman
how surgery might prolong by twenty
the days she could look out her window—
and how drifting out of life
she might hear his screams for warmth—
how his faint belch of content
and milk
might combine with her faint gasp
into death.

7

Yet over the image
of the woman's silence
a montage flashes:
you
          beside another bed:

as your father leaves
your mother whispers   "Why?"
the back door slams forever—

though licking a stick of candy
your tears matched your mother's—
inside   they seeped for years:
you were the thing
                          sucked out and hollow.

8

Till now   this red Monday of October
beside the bed of your unknown son
you know again what you knew

    in the backyard
    in the foxhole
    in the warm kitchen
    in the cold crowd
    in a hospital
    in your mother's arms:

that the body of yourself is the cell of a prison

until you touch another   and know your own flesh
until you look within eyes   and see your own eyes mirrored
until you listen for the pain of another
             and surprised   hear your own pain

           diminish
as it echoes through the open and endless rooms of
               the hearts of them.

YELLOW BIRDS

for John

I'm the captive of a huge man in camouflage—
the skeleton of a human hand around his neck
he shoves me through the brush
                              &
the flock of yellow birds   (lemon   dazzling
some with striped black wings)   glides   hovers—
one huddles between my chin   collarbone
clings to my throat   pulsates:
                              my pet
I remember the way Guatemala looked—
Lake Atitlán   Panajachel   the moonlit
paths toward Mama's   where we drank cerveza
Quitzelteca   ate roast chicken   chiles—
the cool tiles   the incense   as we danced
to the South American folk band
                              & dear
no one   with however many submachine guns
handcuffs   flayed bones   can take away this moment
this one yellow bird quivering   *blessing   blessing.*

THE WILD BIRDS

Weighted by a languor I would crash
I watch the spare green dogwood blooms
   hover over redbirds on the grass.
From on low   one rises to my sill—
   the bird and I sit eye to eye
his grave artless bead inquires.
   Desire dissolves the glass between:
to part his radiant thicket   to
   plunge beneath covers of red   to touch
the fevered mound.   & thinking my hand
   amid his quiver of barb and quill
my palms unclasp within my lap.

   The bird flies down to mince   to dance
to wait.   & I watch   through the frame
   myself run to gather birds: one
bitter thrashing armful.   Birds cry
   claws rush toward my hair   my dress
the dizzy wingshafts scrape my breast.
   Yet now   my fingers grasp the arc
of pulse   the frame of bones   the shape
   that cradles the wild bird.   & as birds ball
to dense red   I watch my body fall
   beneath feathers & sharp yellow kisses—
the mouth of my face smiles   disappearing—
   I see myself die for passion: willing.

THE COLOR OF HALCYON DAYS

The days are drops of cream
that fall from a cream-colored pitcher
onto a dull gray plate.   &

the gray of the plate is tender
wraps around all intensity—
a warm kind of coat for pain
a soft kind of fluff to numb.

A white horse alone in the field
a miniature to hold in my palm
moves with slow-motion limbs—

the animal rolls with the ground
the gray of a tree trunk is static
an egg yolk quivers on porcelain:
the pale form will break and run.

Yet at two in the afternoon
all is cream in my kitchen & soul—
the color of peace is monochrome.